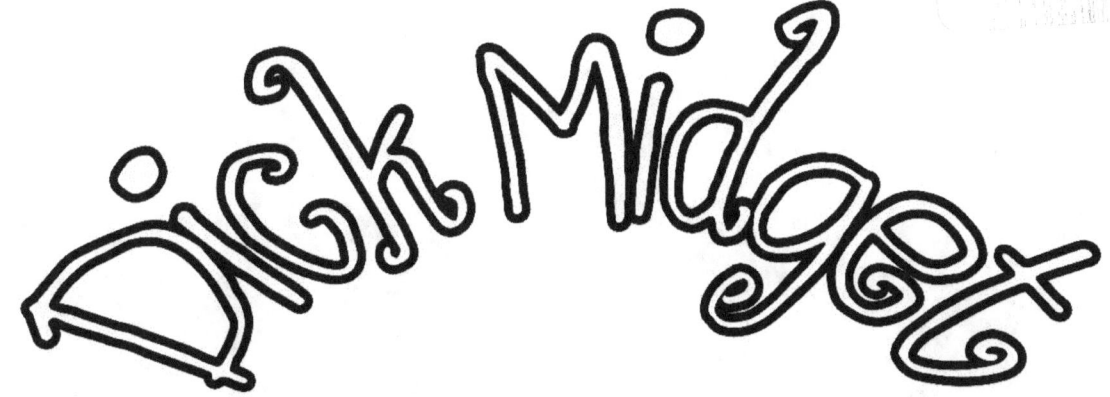

Dick Midget

FLORIST SWEAR

Wondrous Swear Word To Color

For Stress Releasing

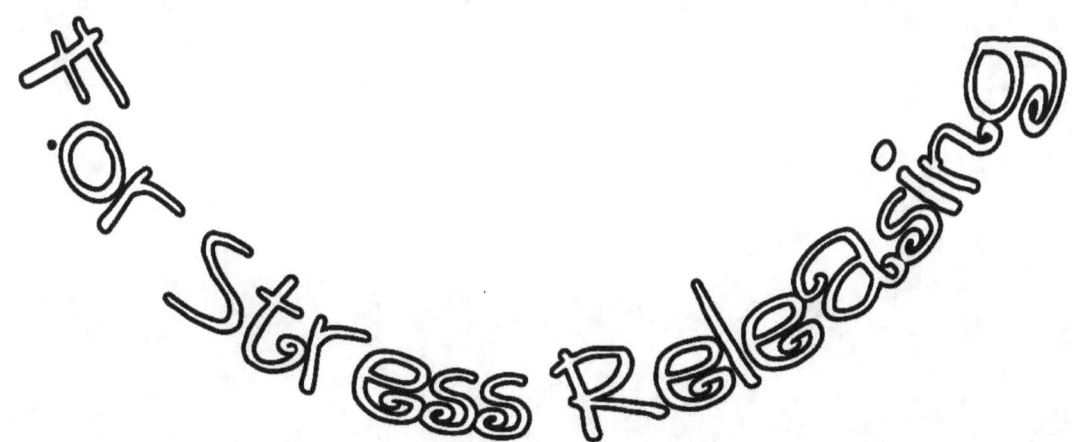

Charity Borsberry

Happy Coloring!

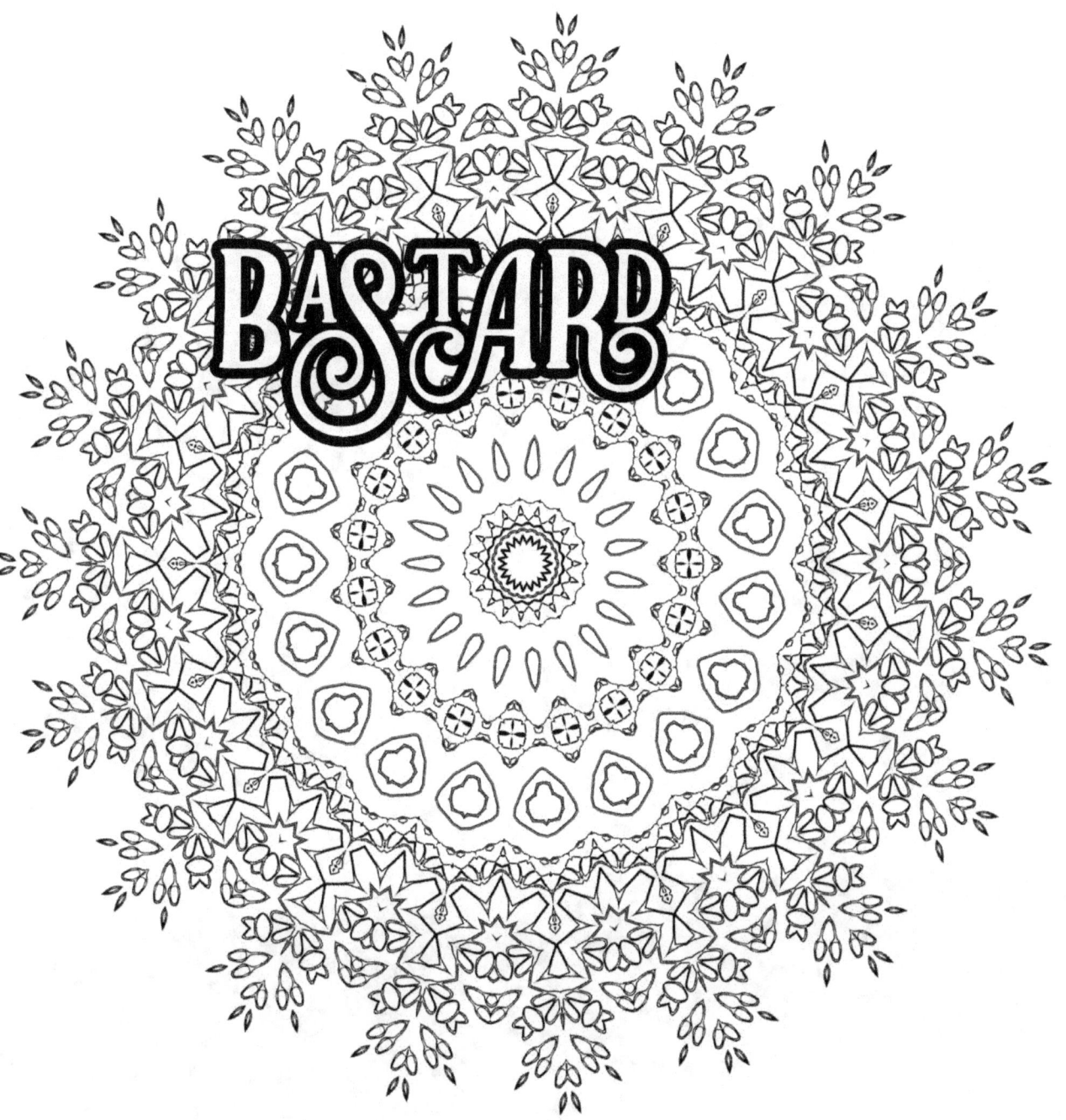

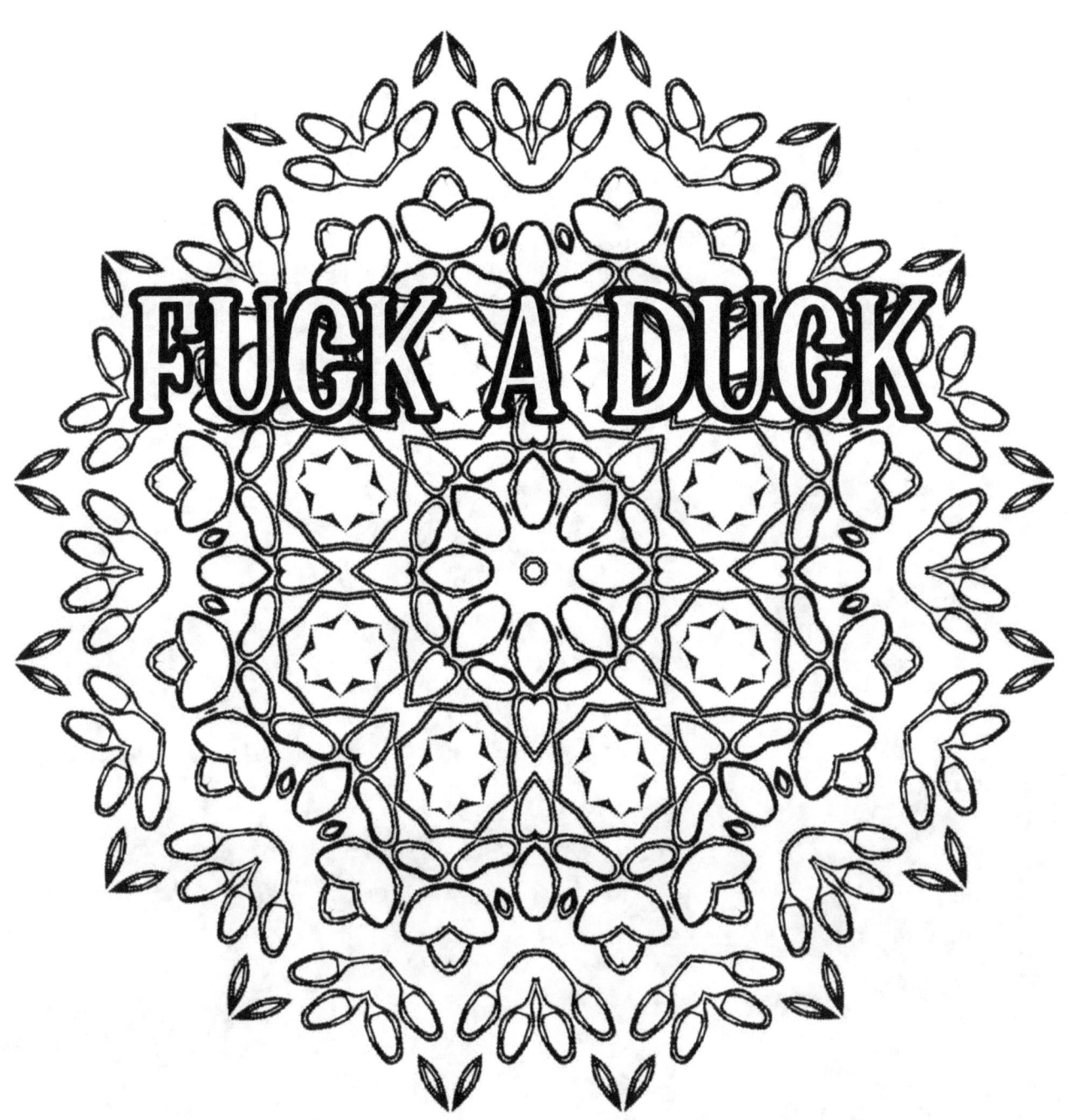

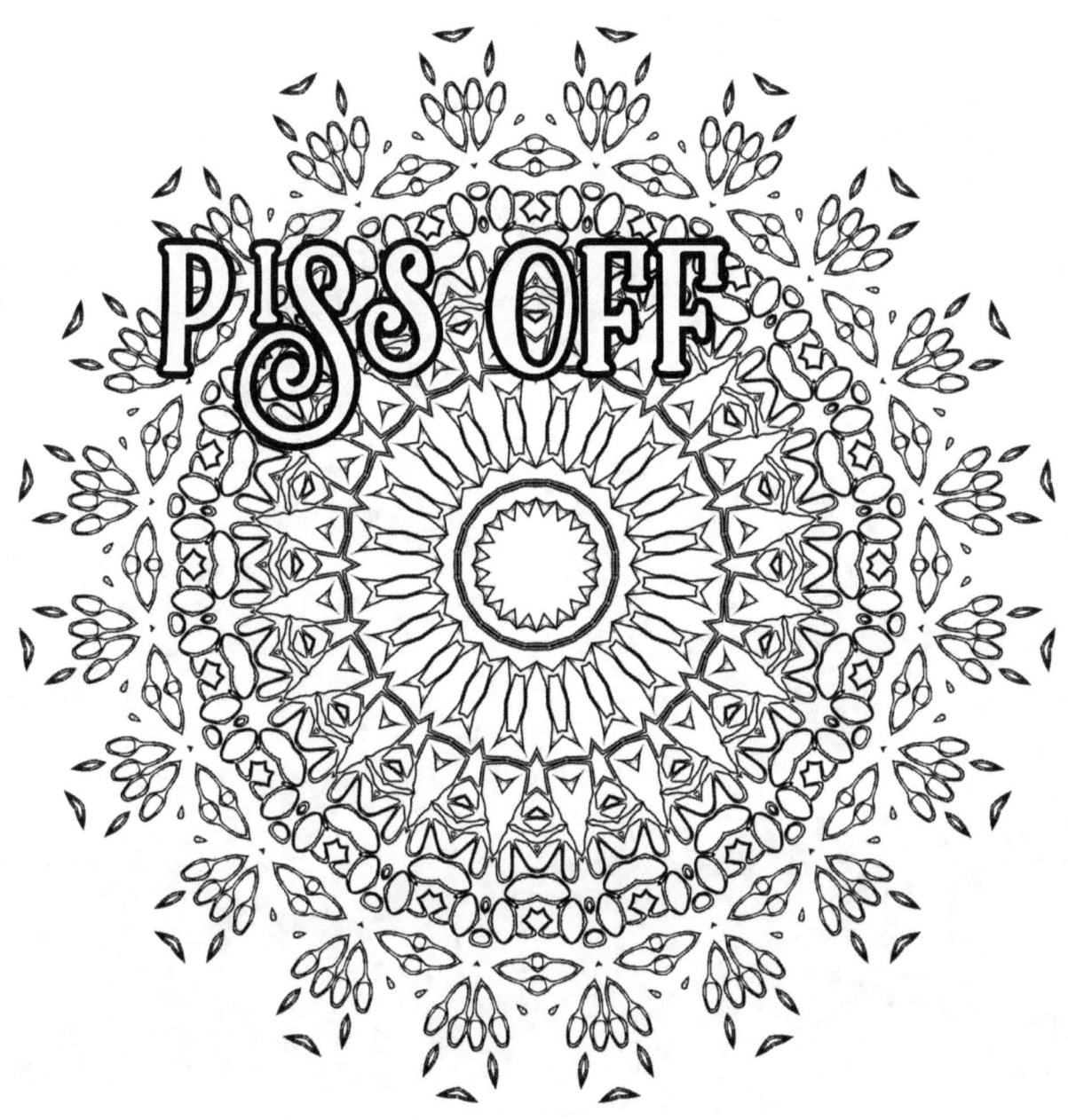

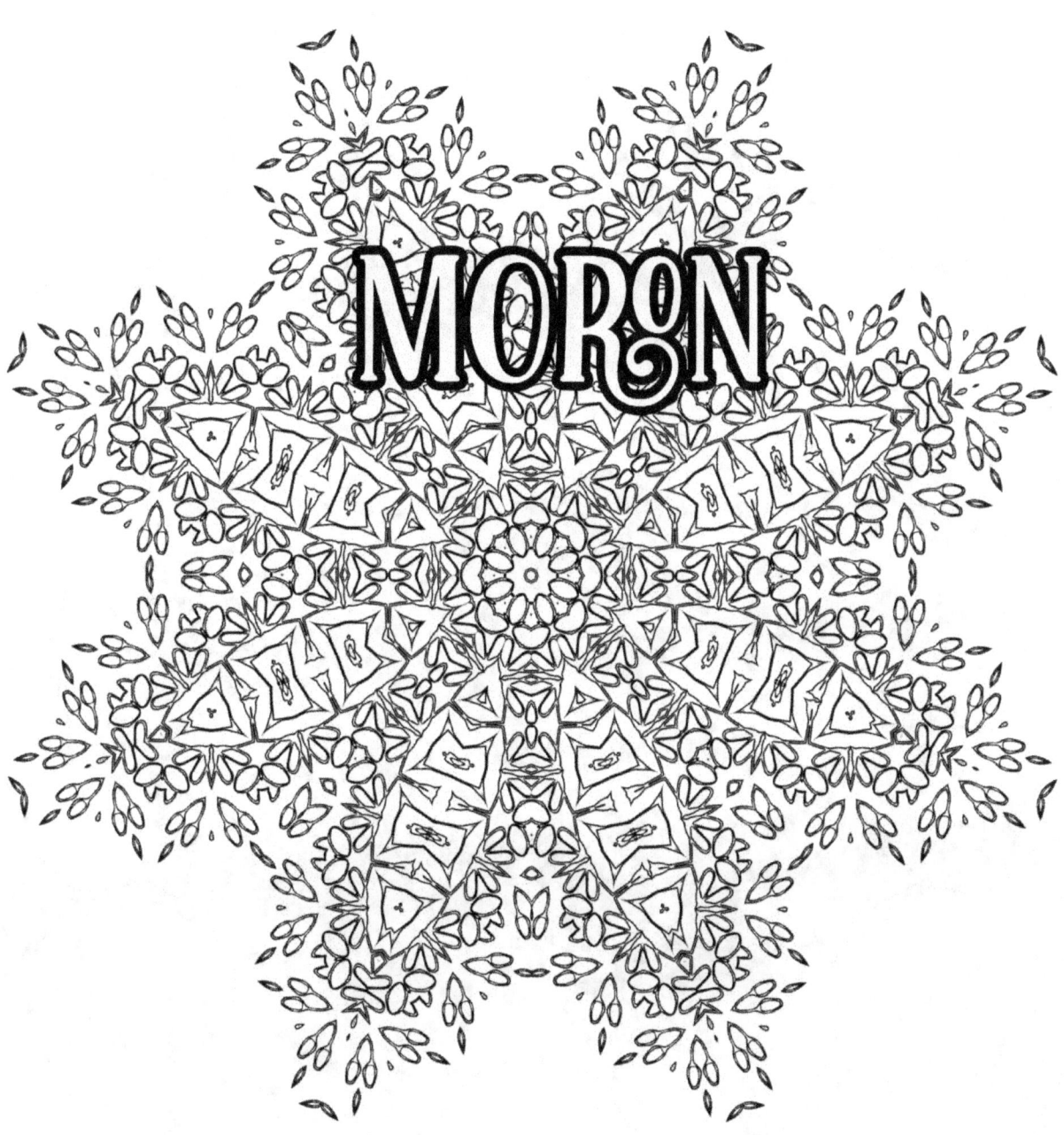

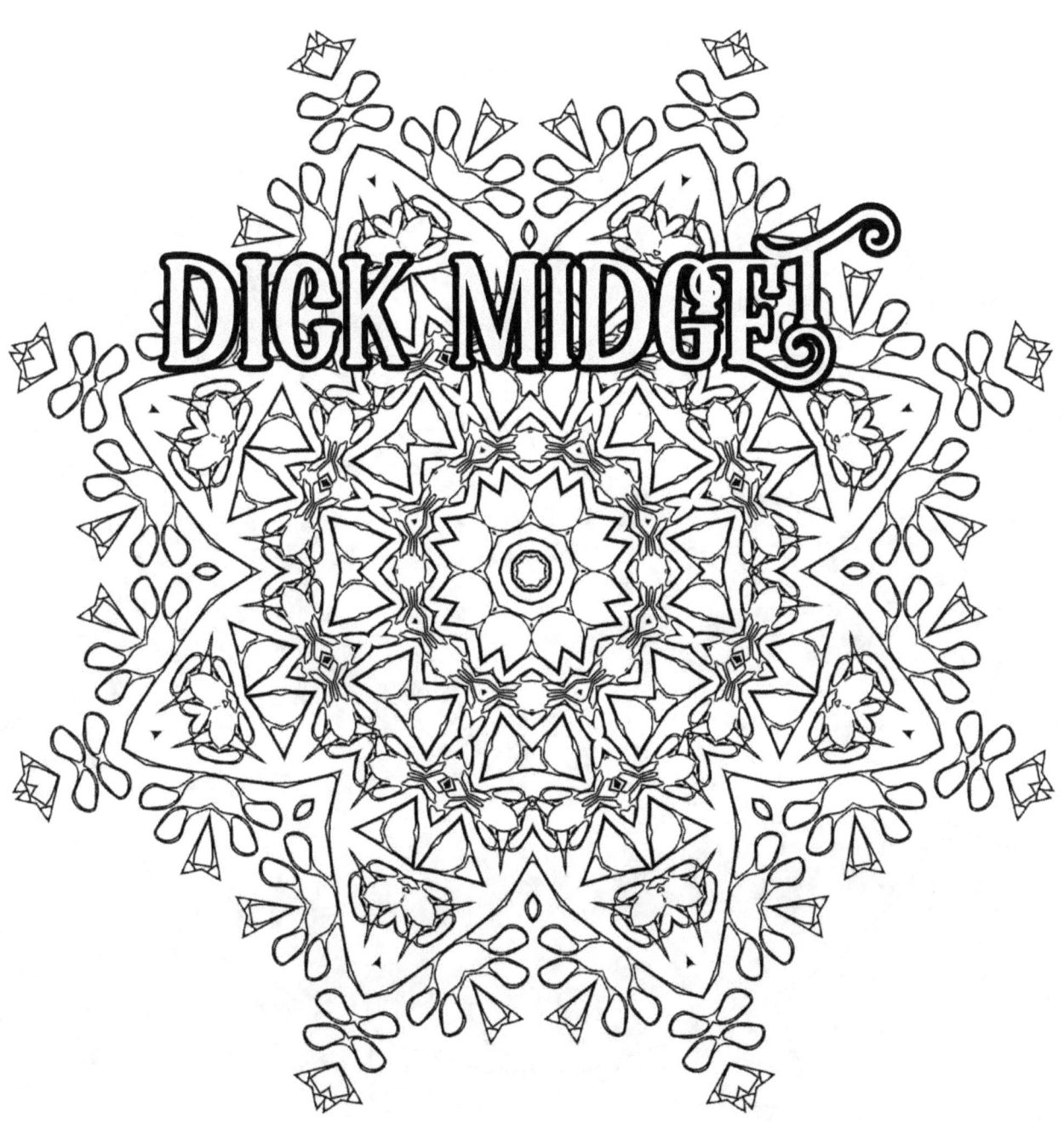

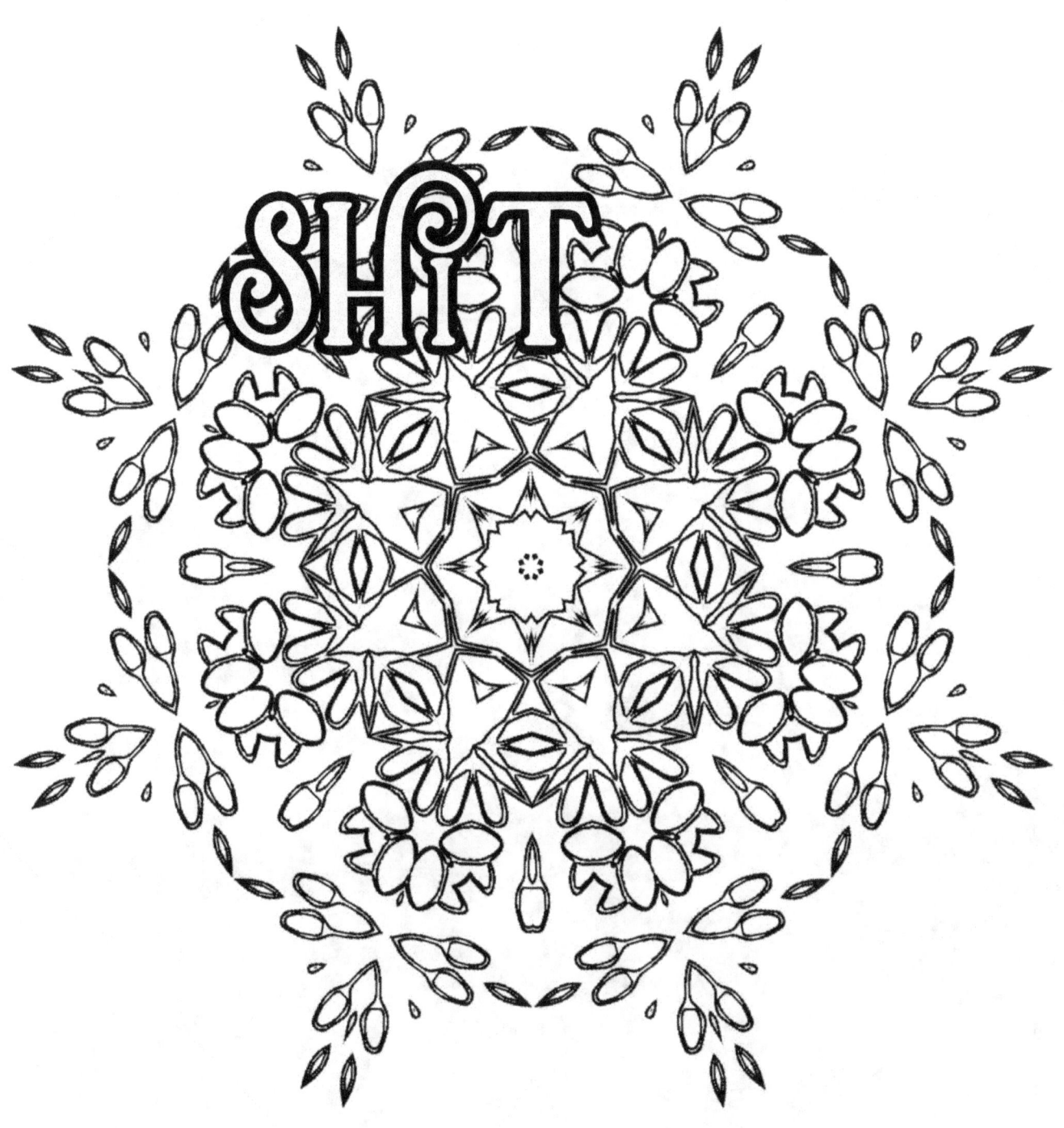

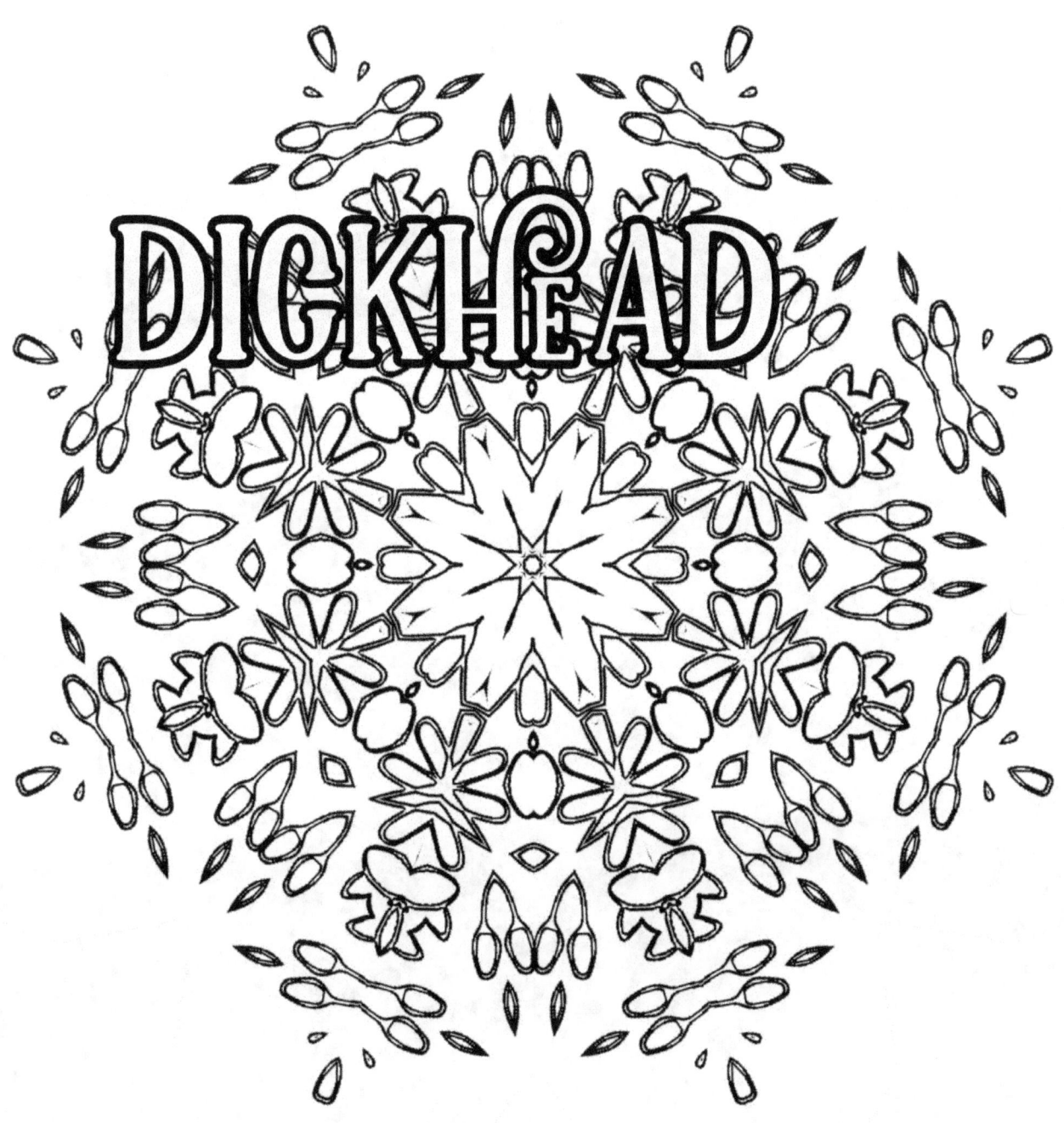

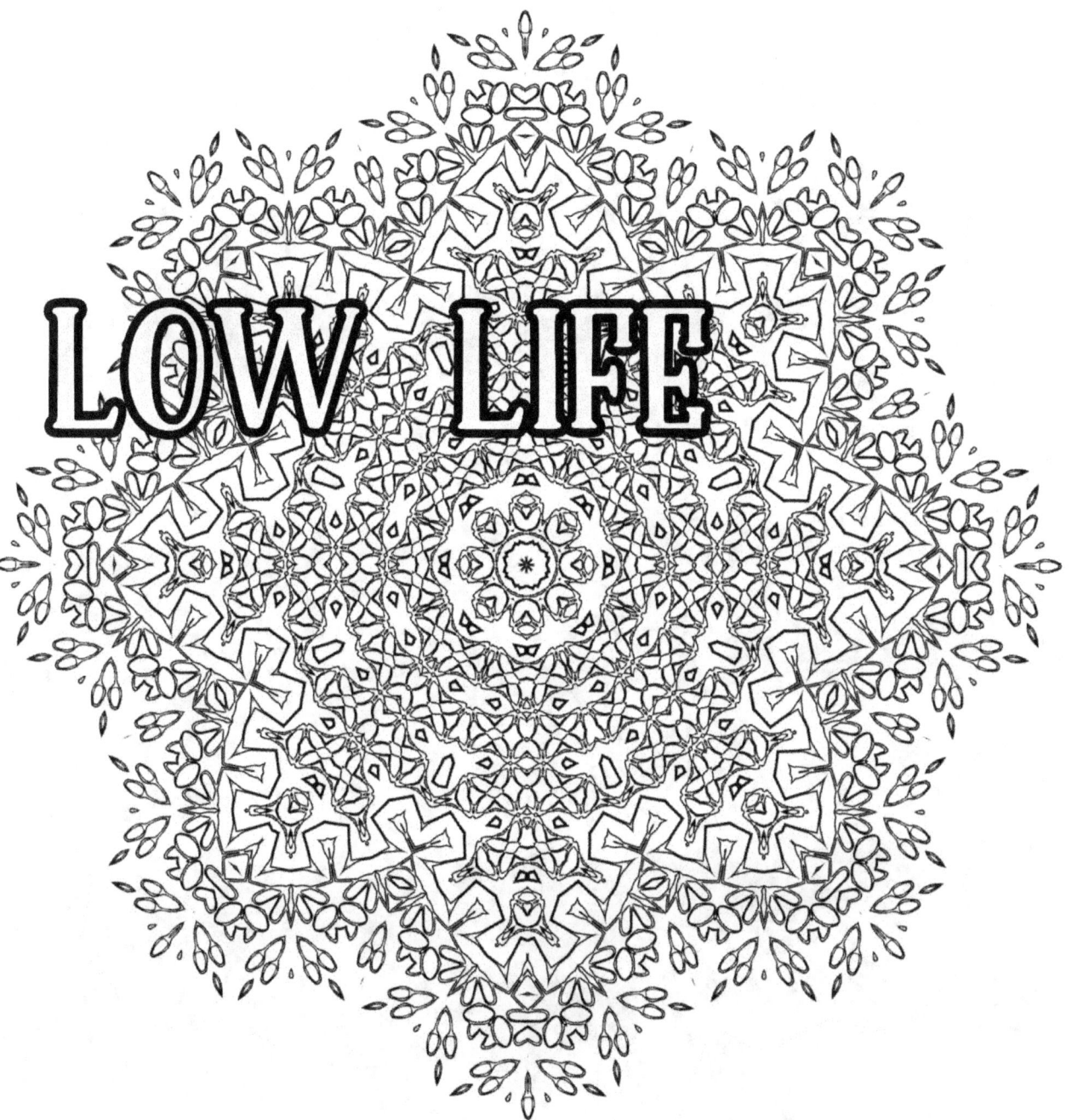

LOW LIFE

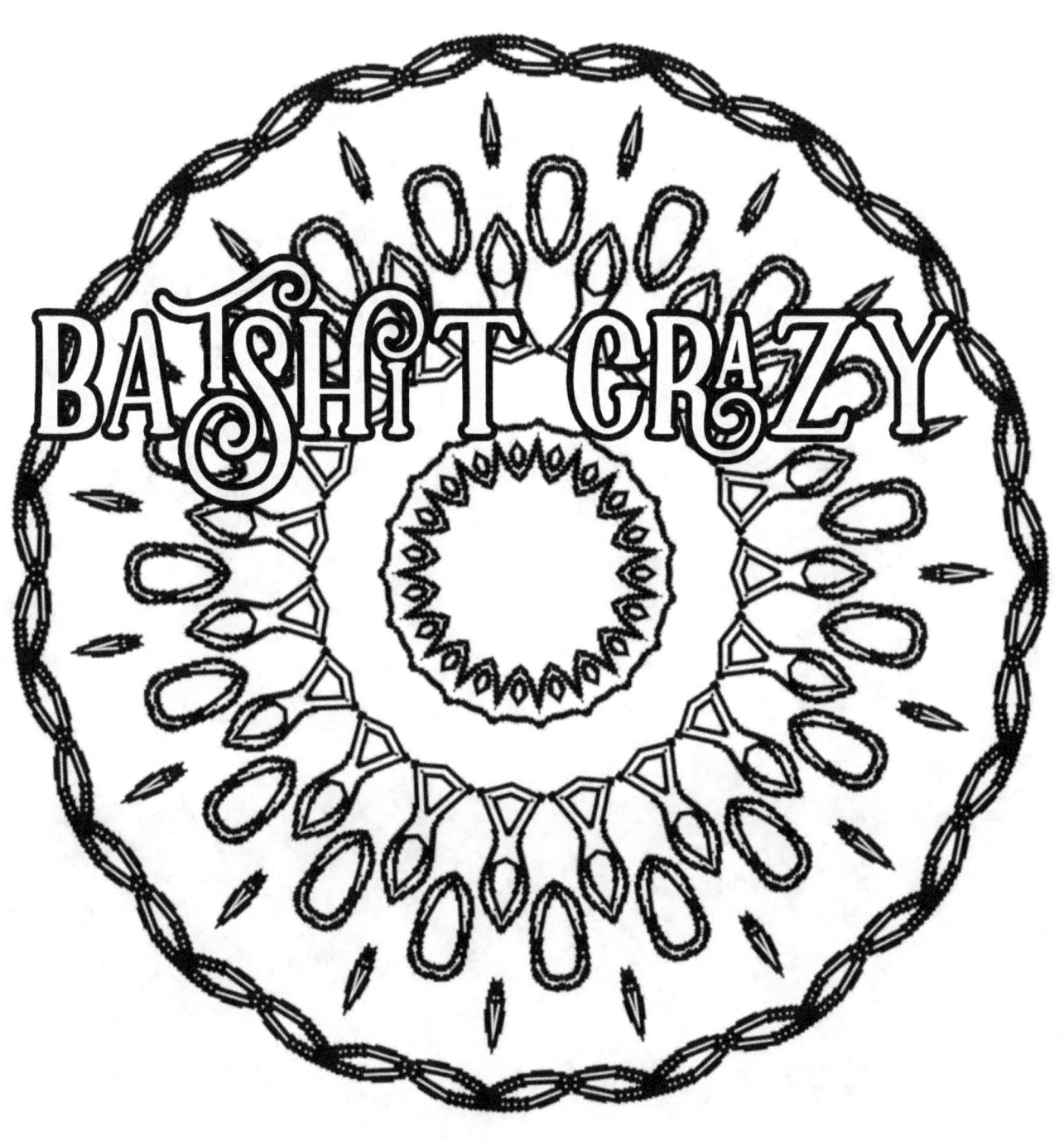

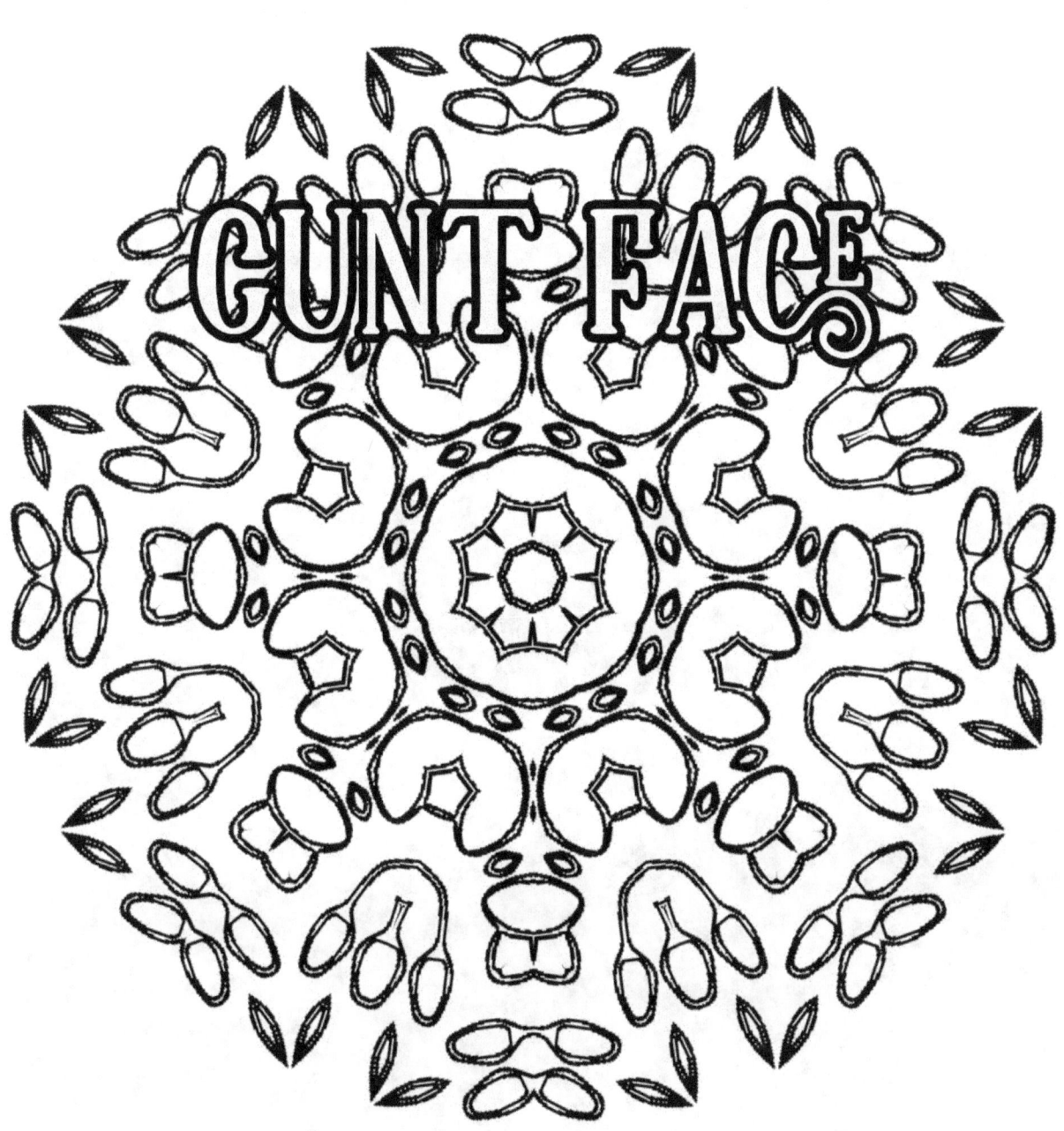

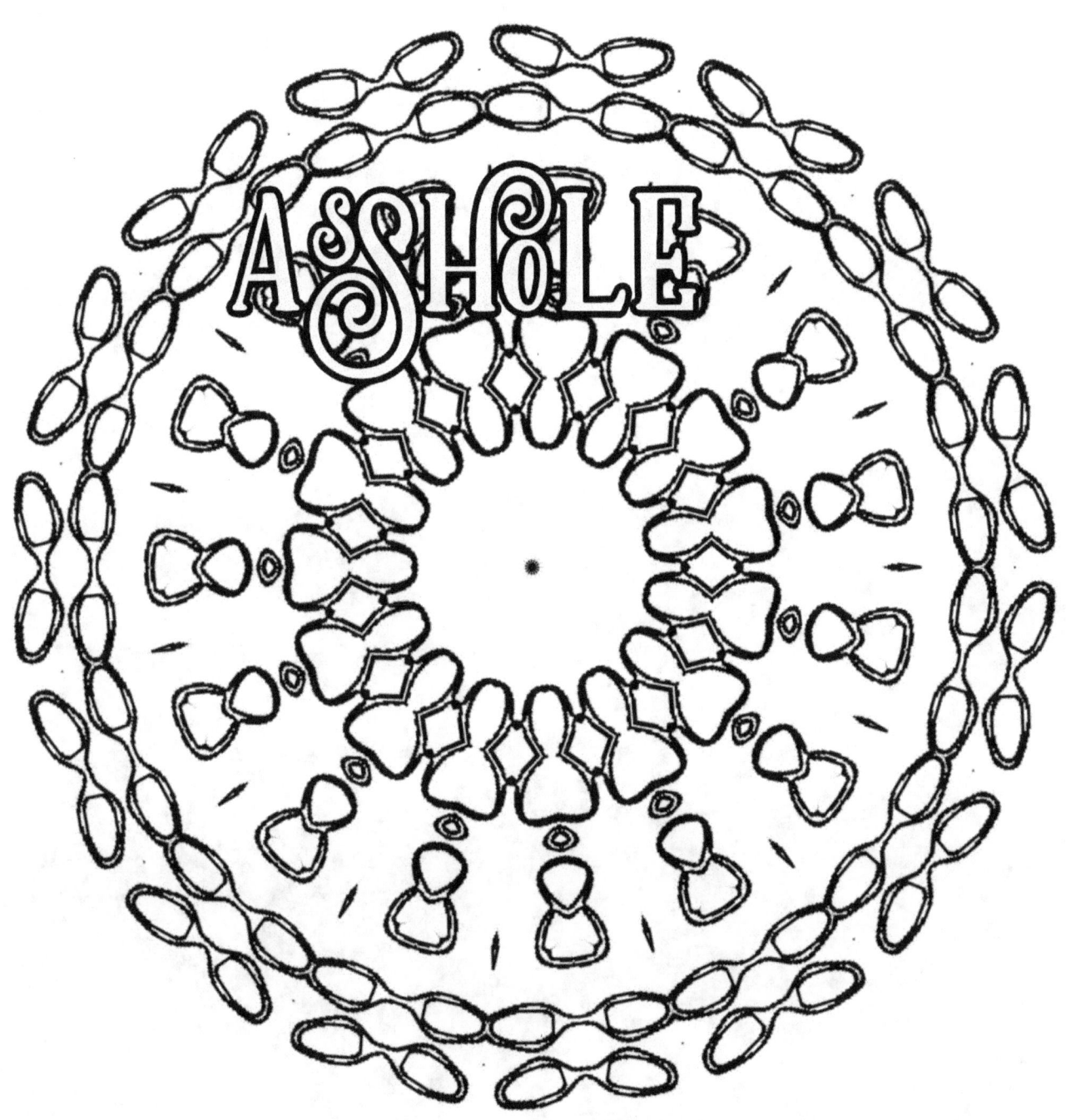

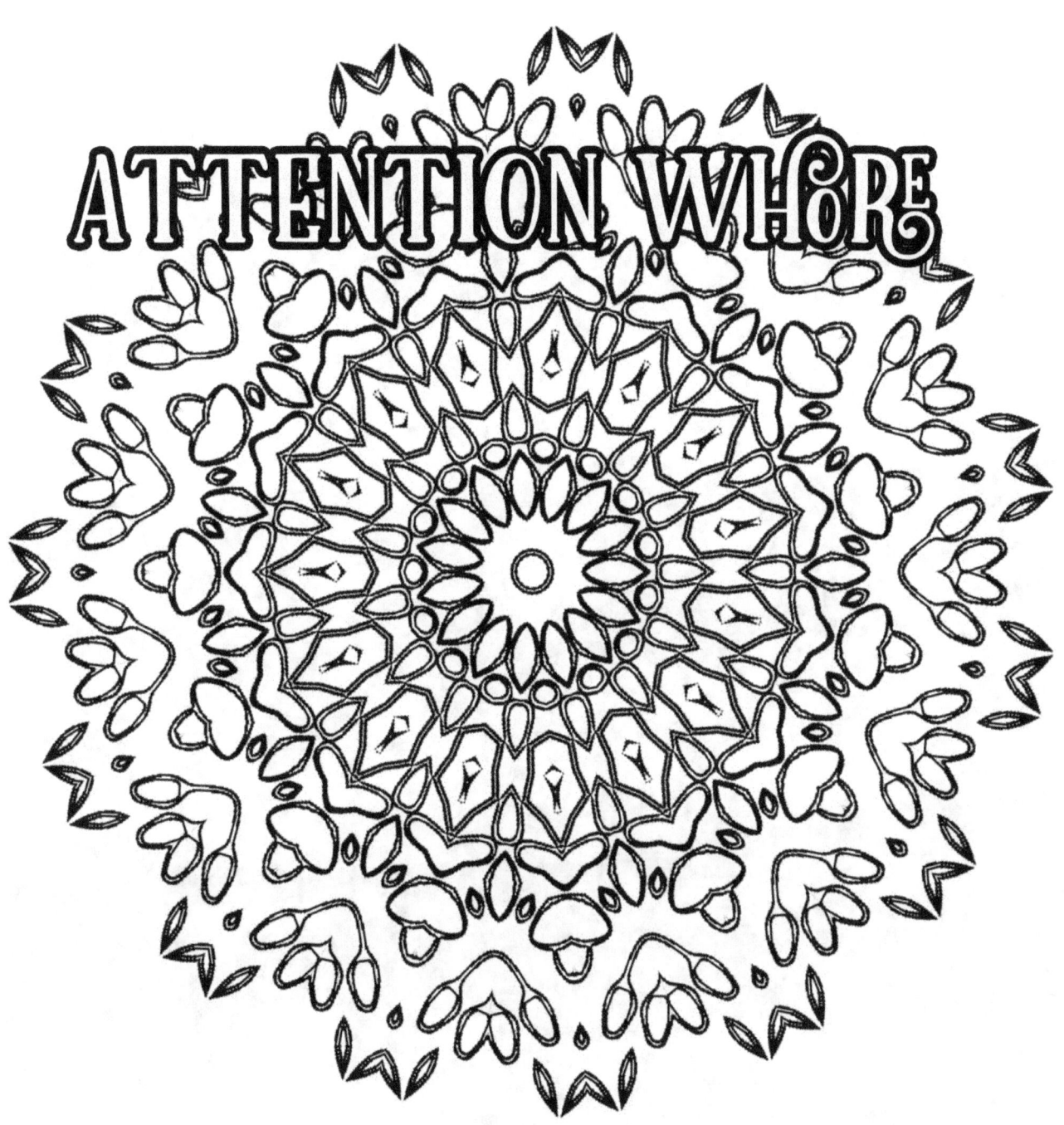

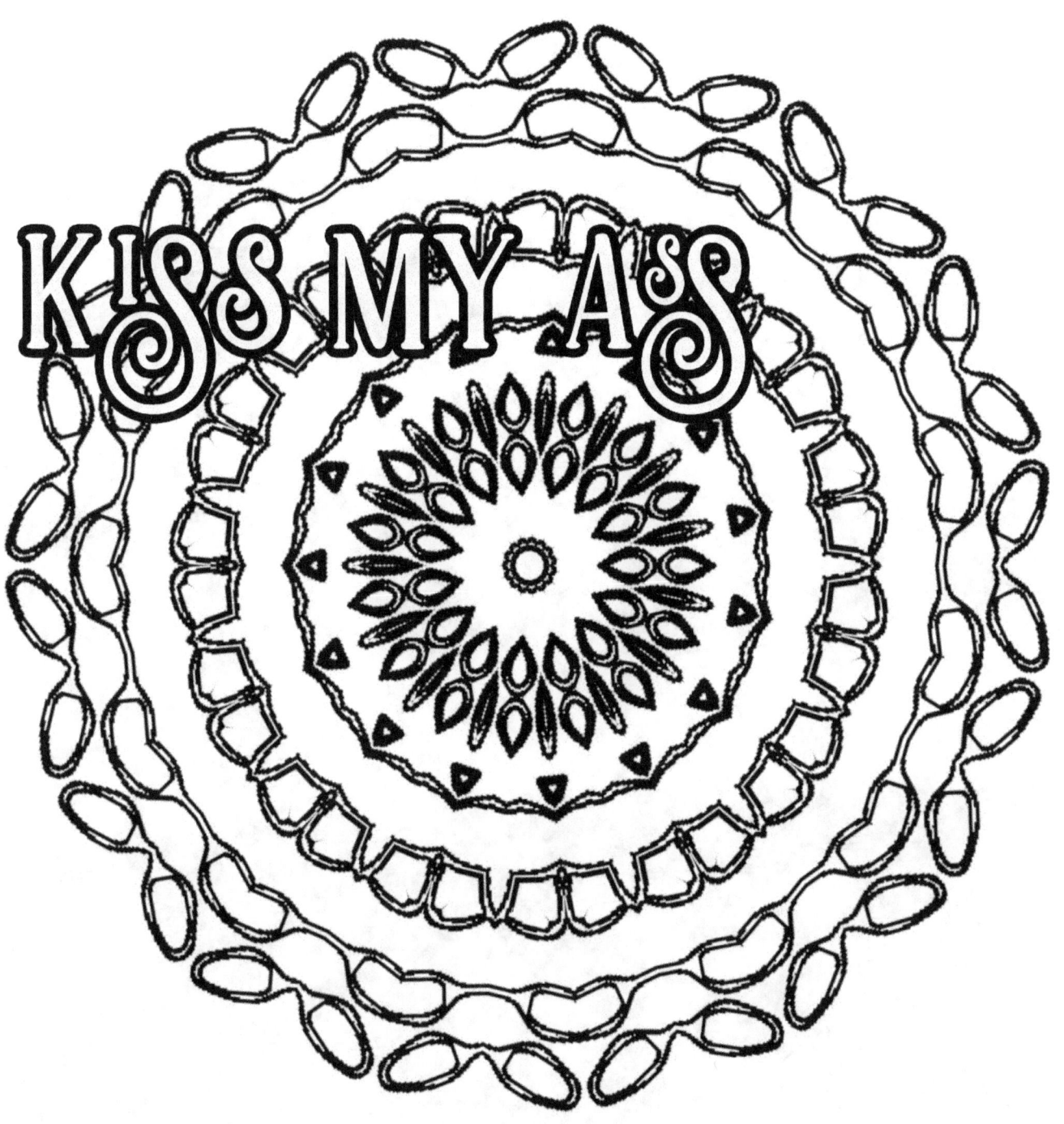

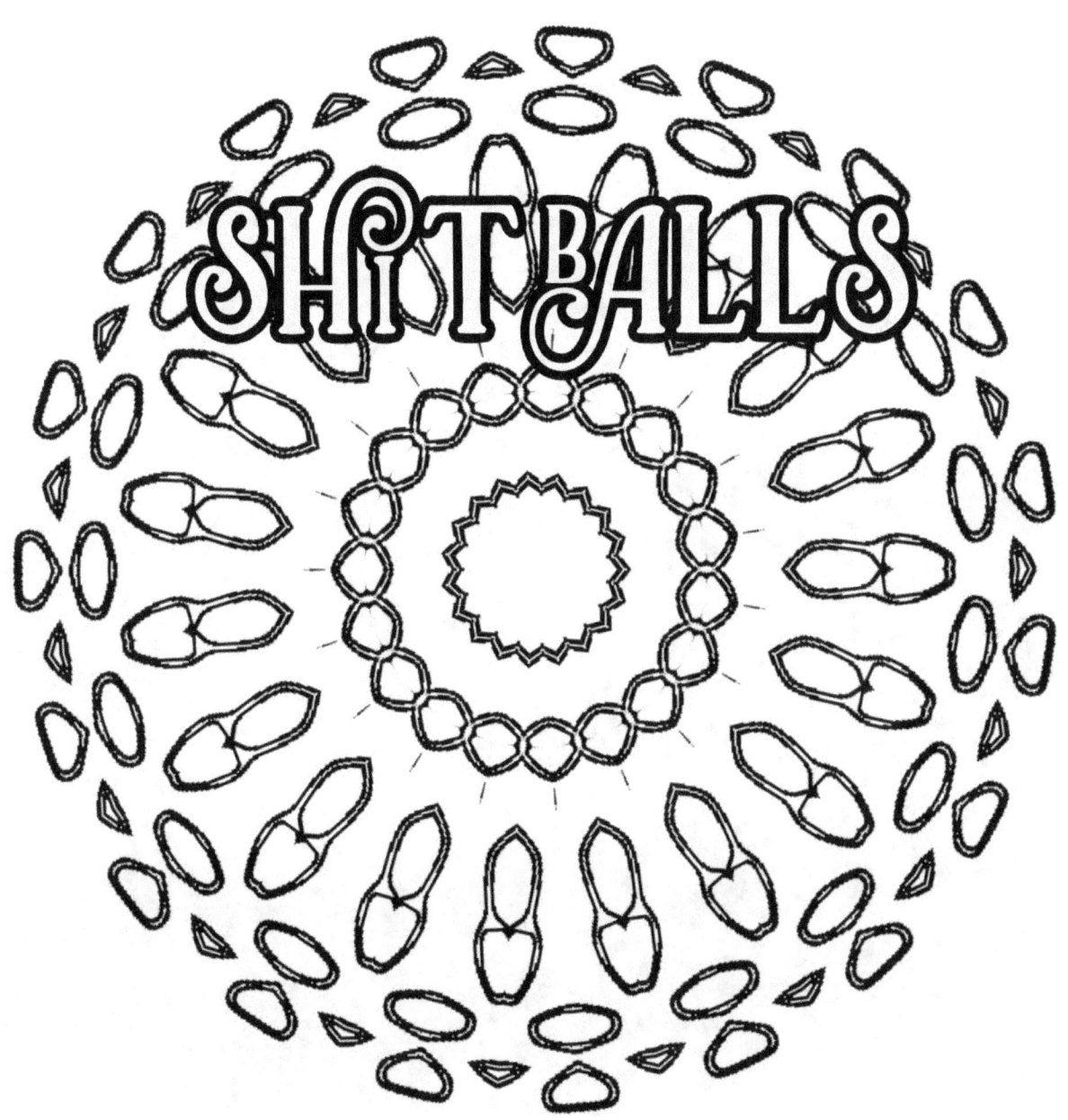

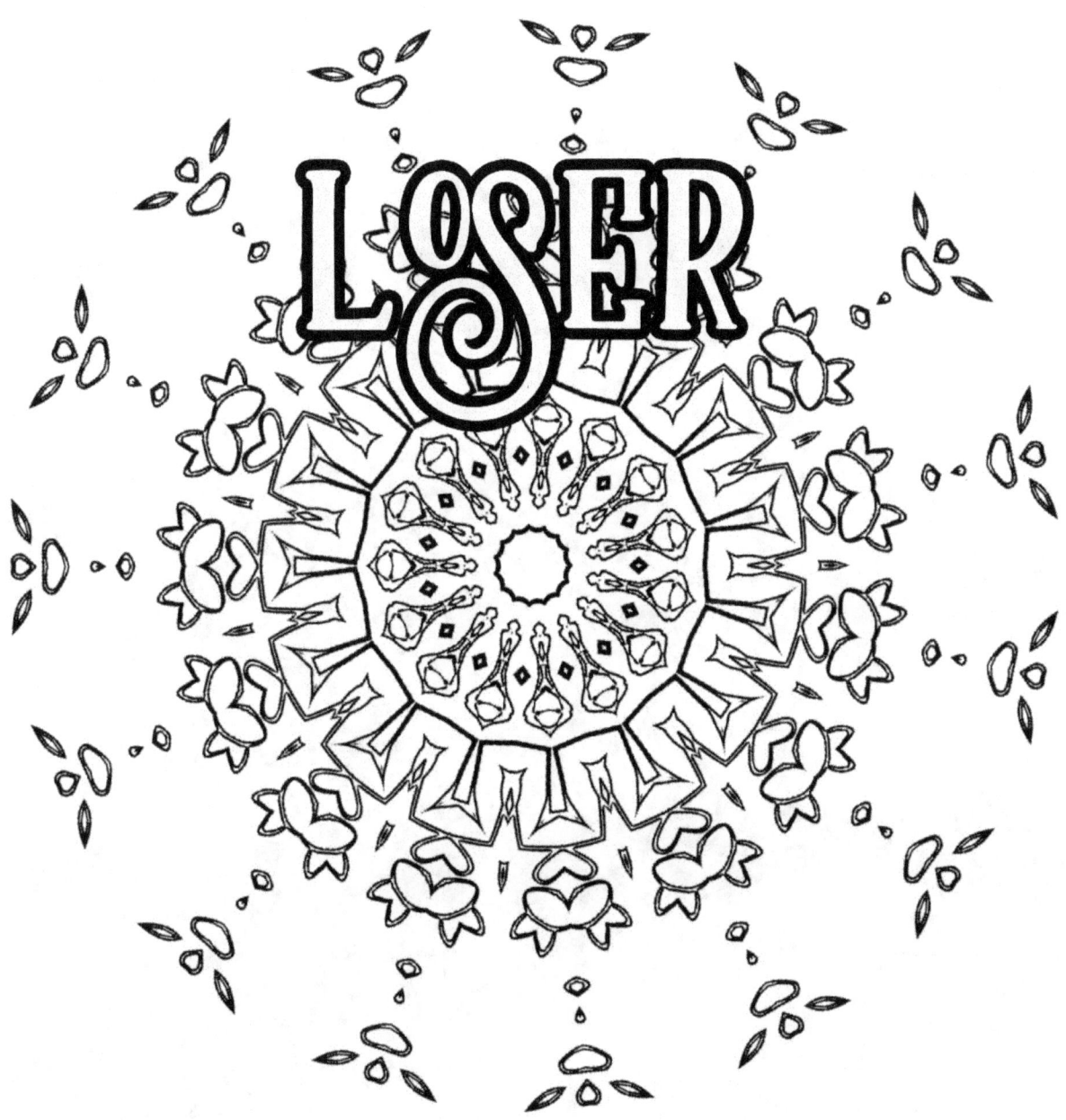

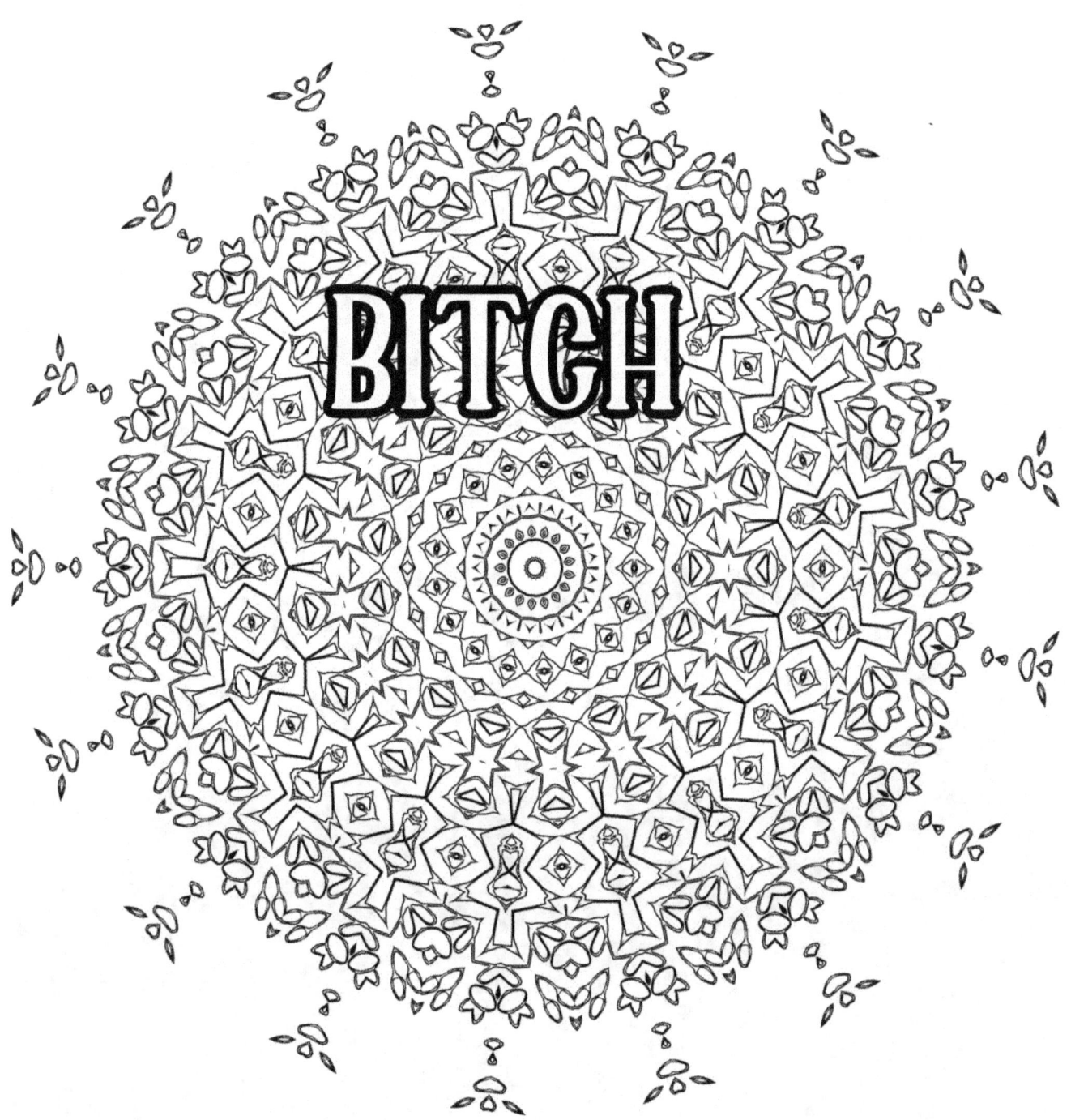

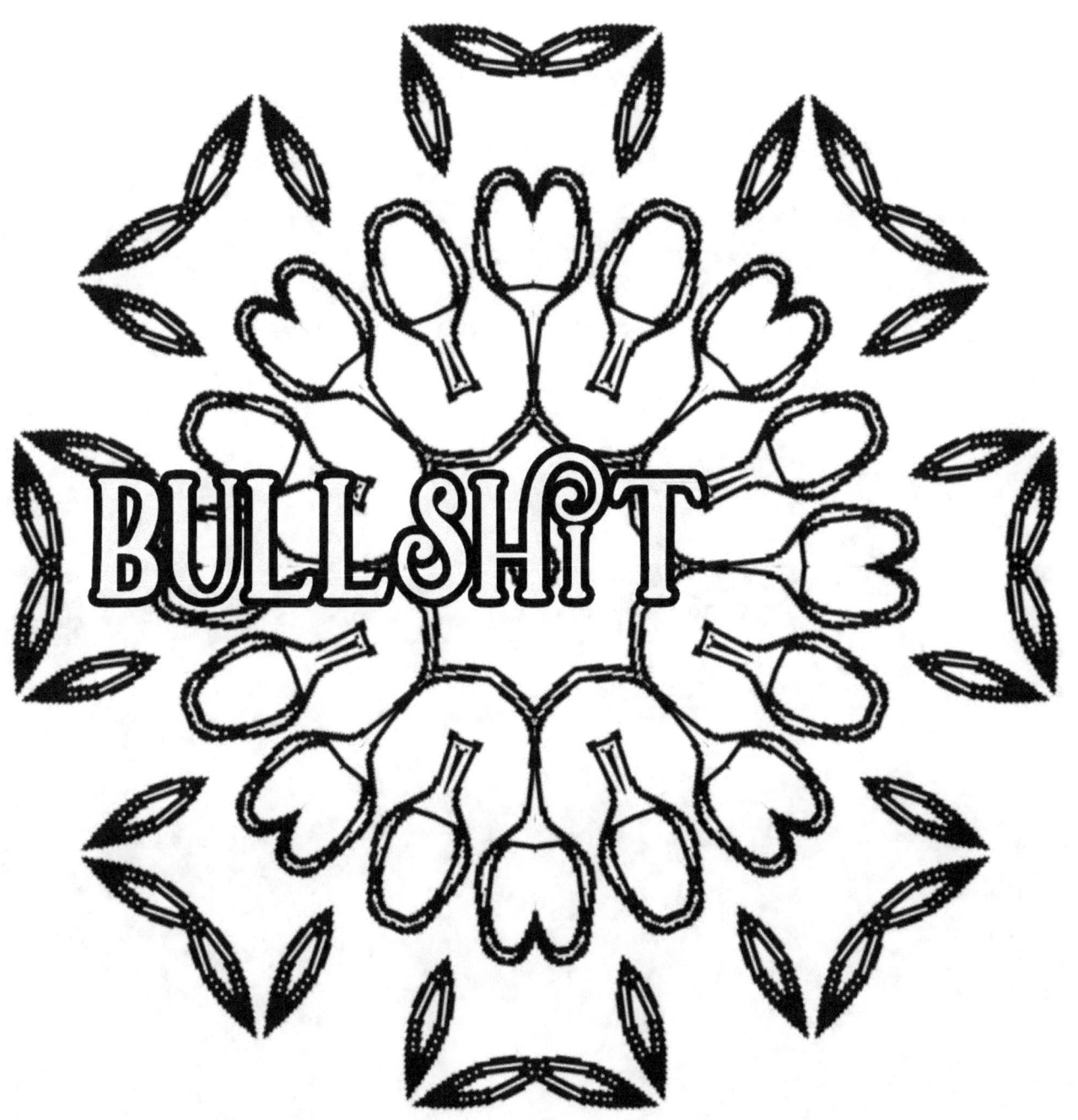

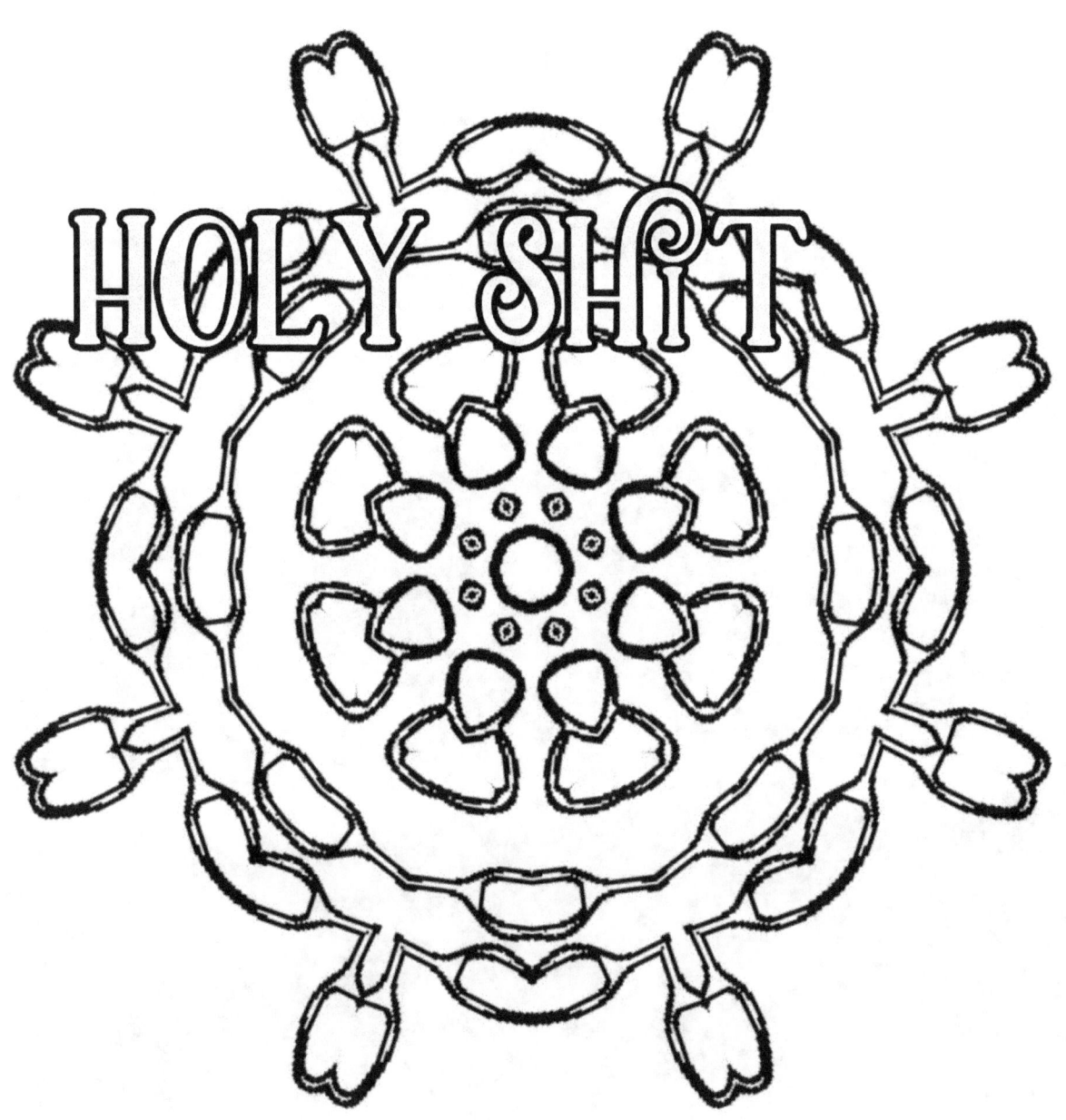

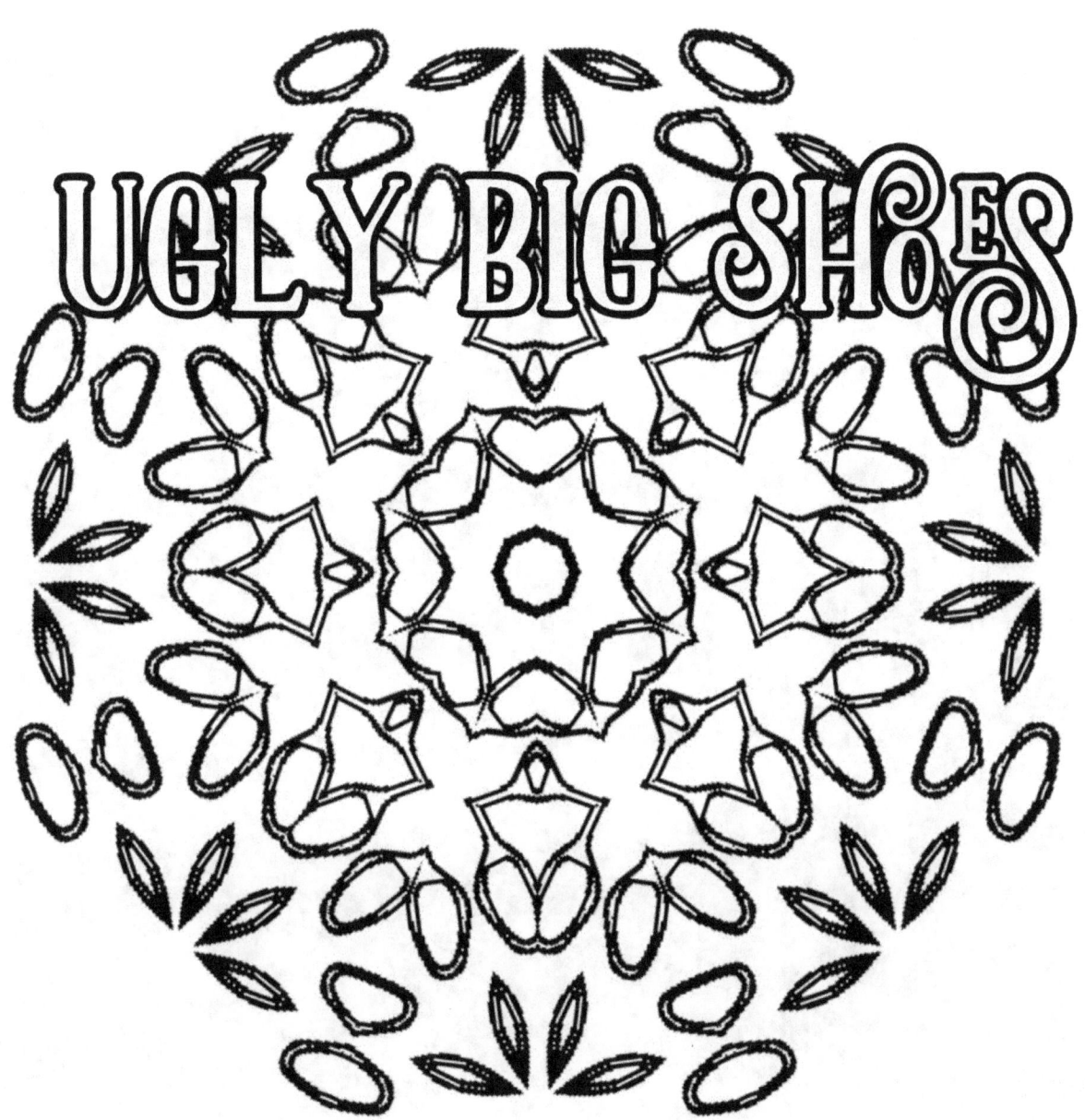

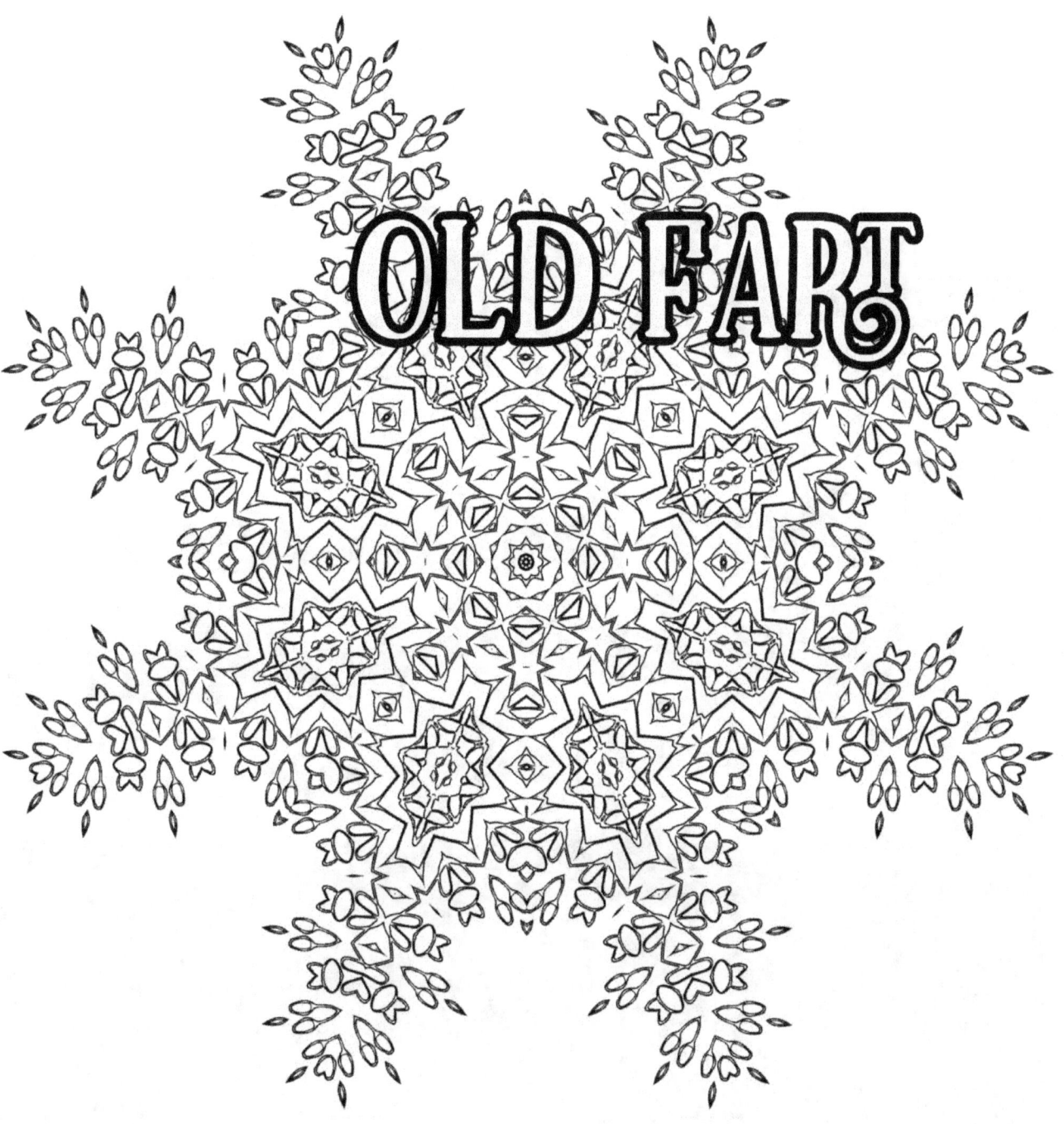

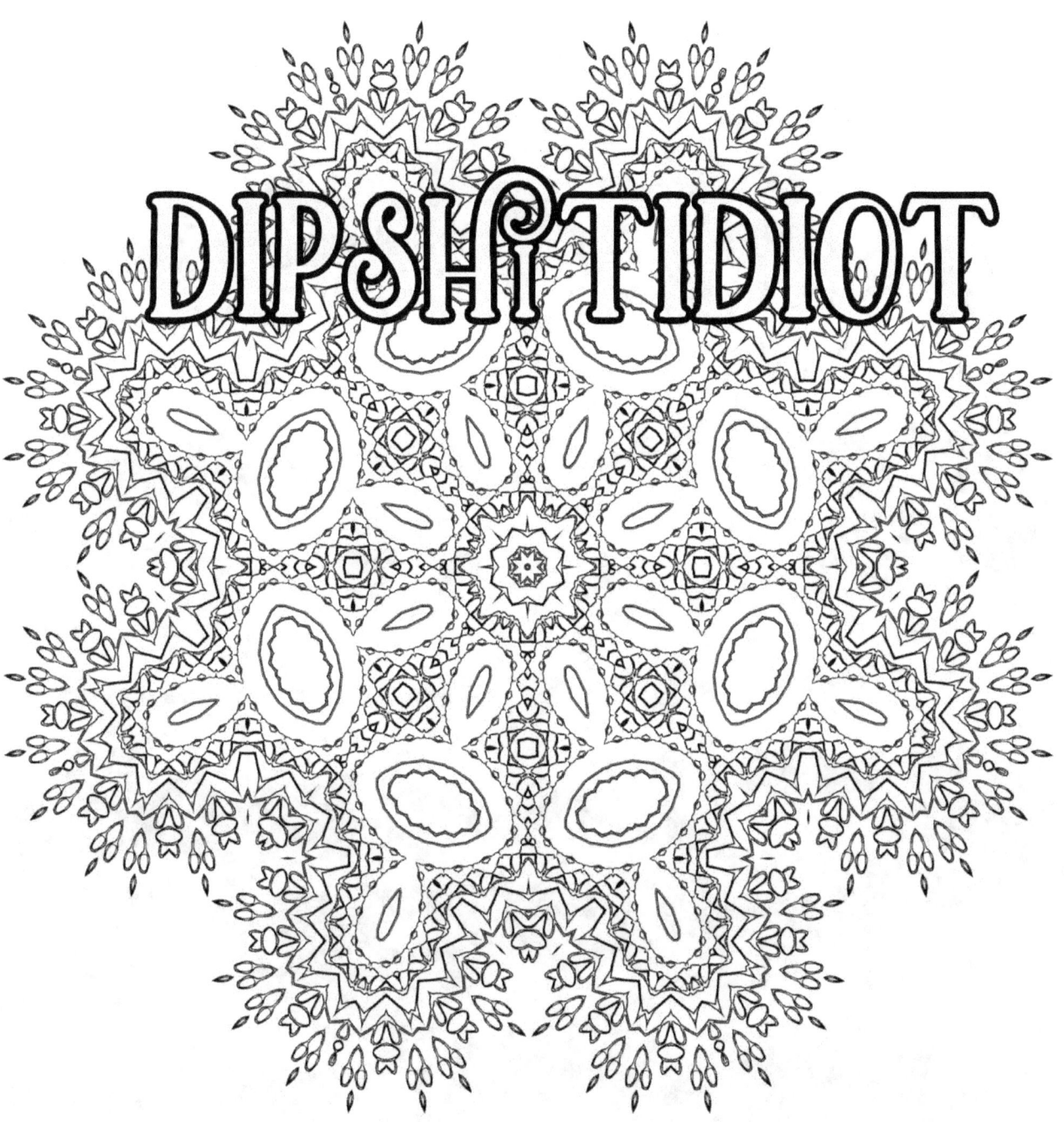

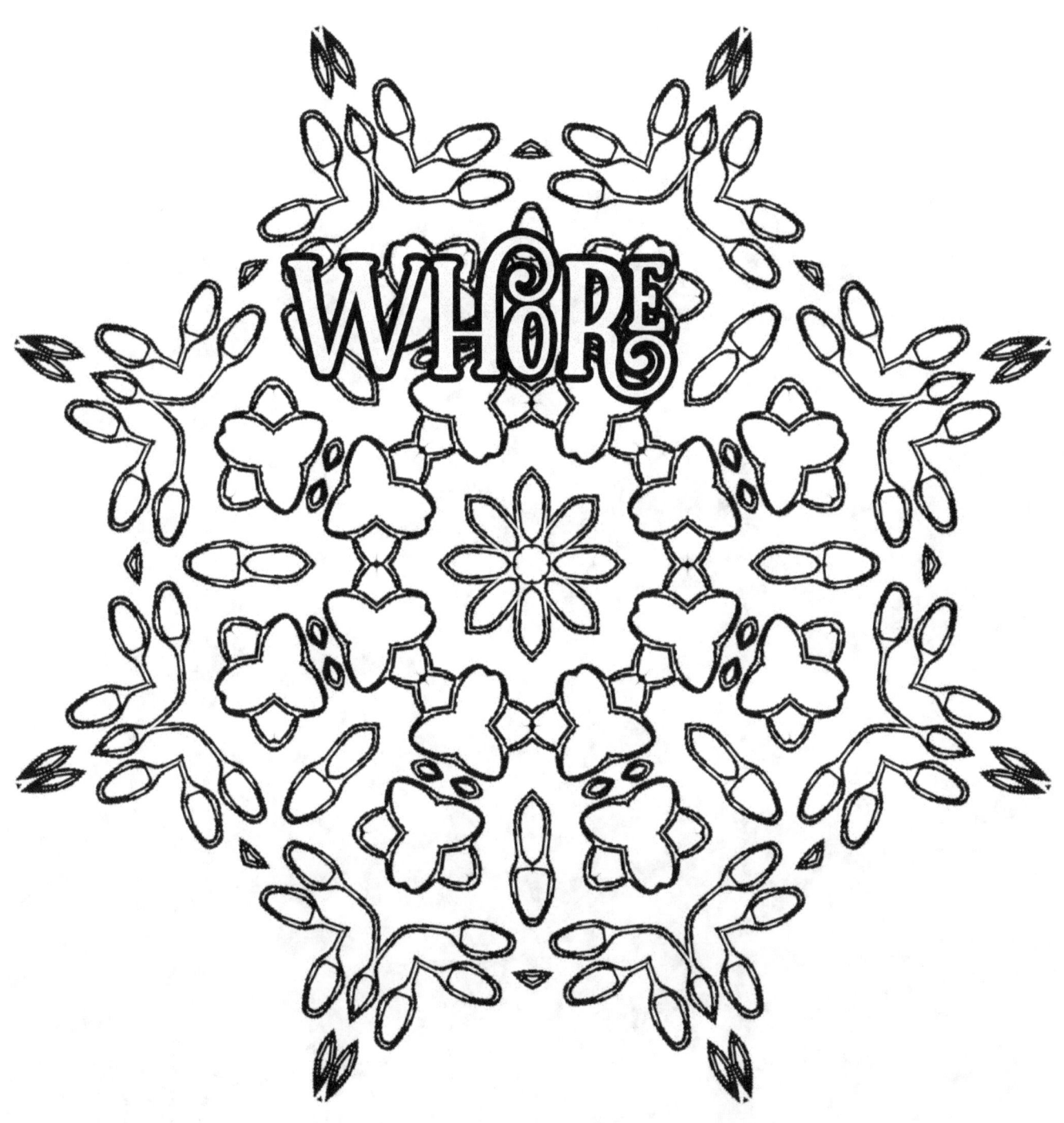

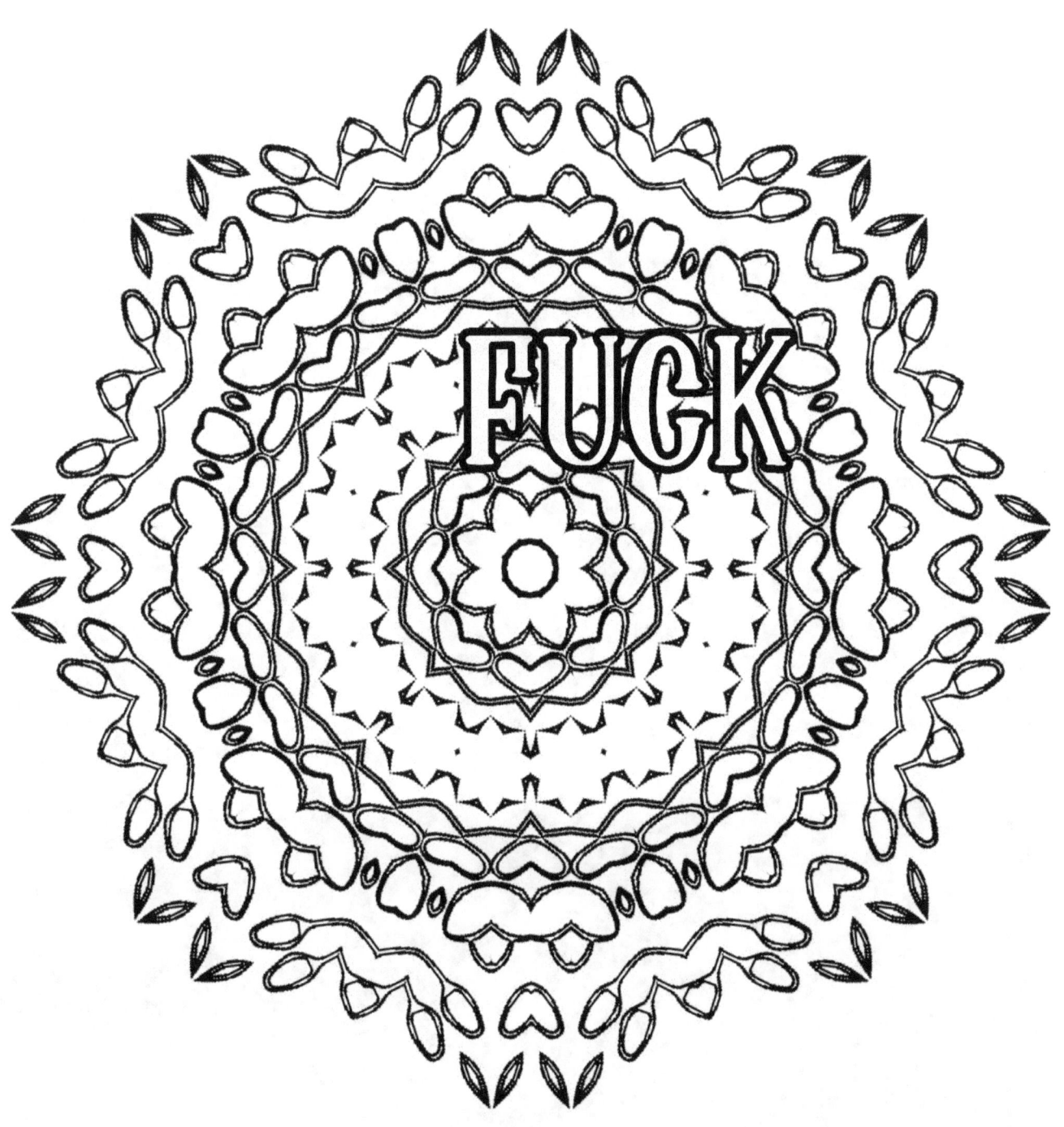

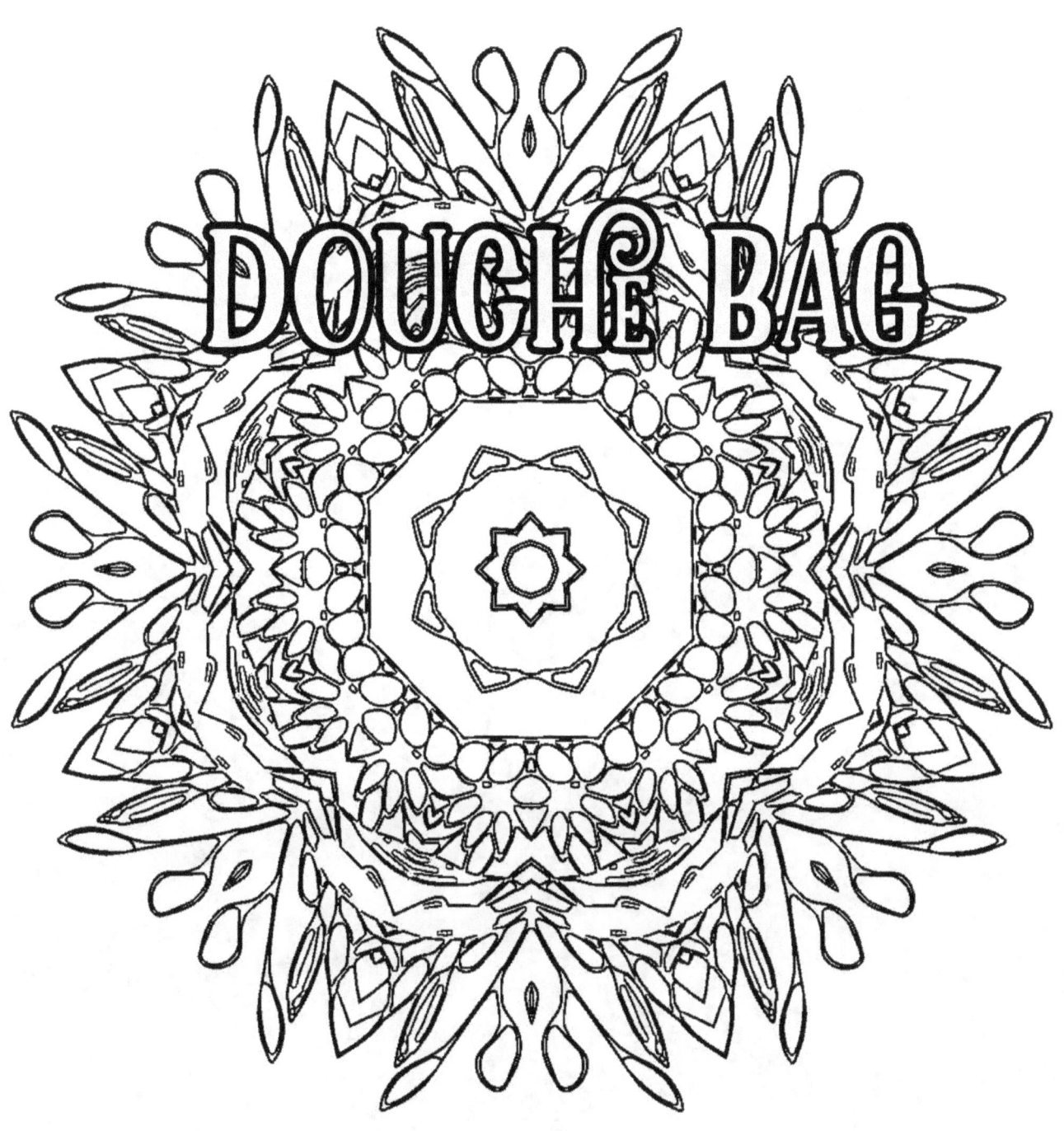

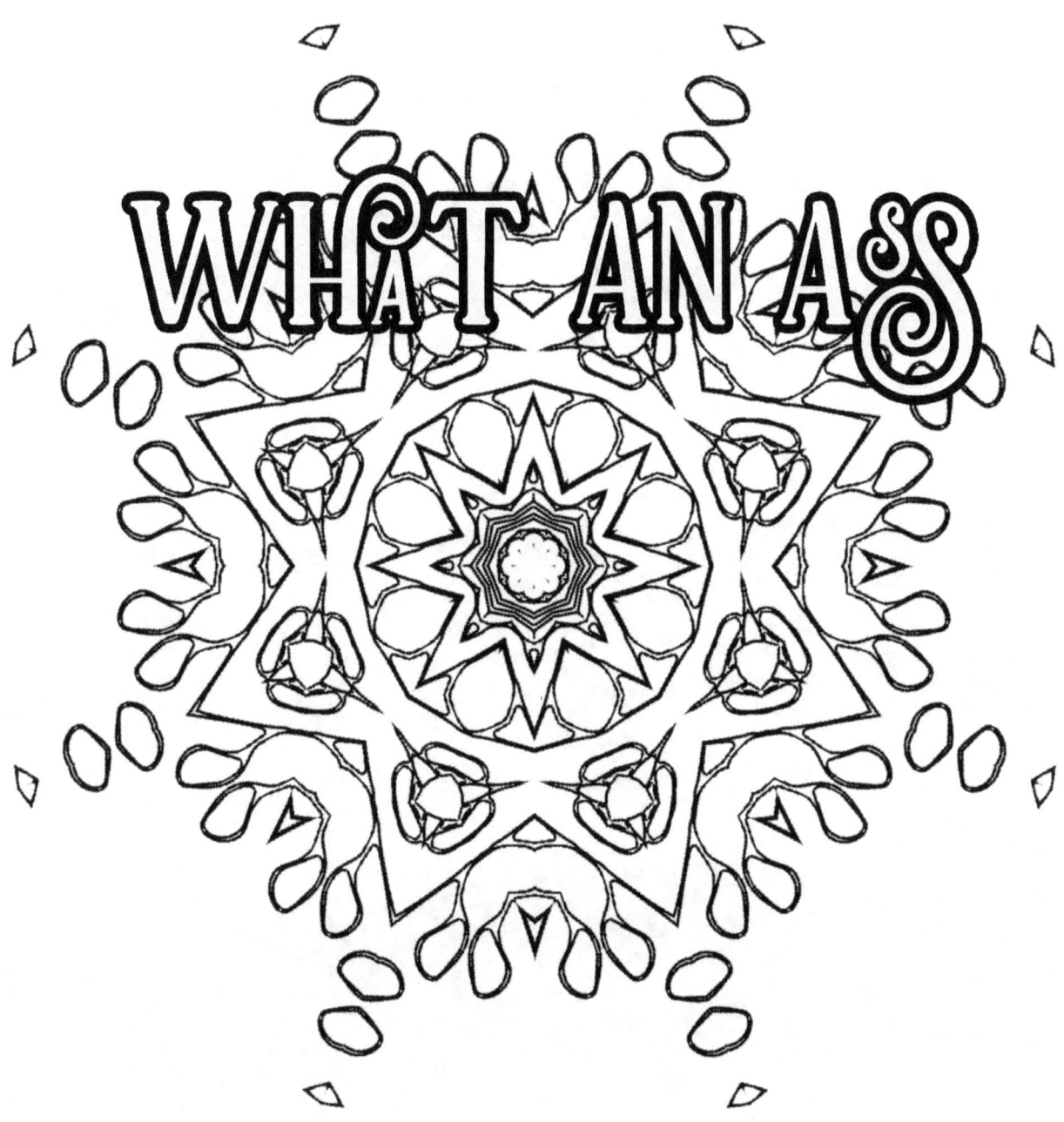

www.ingramcontent.com/pod-product-compliance
Lightning Source LLC
Chambersburg PA
CBHW081748170526
45167CB00009B/3969